HOPE FOR TOMORROW

A Prayer Guide for North Korea

Copyright © 2012, OMF International

Published by OMF International

10 West Dry Creek Circle, Littleton CO 80120

ISBN-13: 978-1-907736-01-8

ISBN-10: 1-907736-01-8

This printing *2013*

OMF BOOKS

Visit *www.OMFBooks.com* for more information.

STATISTICS

Full name: Democratic People's Republic of Korea (DPRK)

Population: 23, 990, 703

Area: 122,370 sq. km.
*Only 15% of the land is arable.

Capital: Pyongyang
(pop. 2.74 million)

Other major cities:
Namp'o
(pop. 1.1 million)

Urbanites: 63.4%

Population under 15 years old: 22%

Life expectancy: 67.1 years

Peoples
Korean: 99.8%
Chinese: 0.2%

Language
Korean

Religion
Non-religious: 69.3%
Ethnoreligionist: 15.5%
Other: 13.2%
Christian: 1.48%
Buddhist: 0.40%

*Up to 100,000 Christians are interned in labor camps.
*Approximately 300,000 North Korean refugees live in China.

(Source: *Operation World*, 2010)

INTRODUCTION

Though isolated from the rest of the world in many ways, North Korea continues to make headlines. Kim Jong-Il, the "Great Leader," died in December 2011; his young son Kim Jong-Un has succeeded him as the next ruler. April 15, 2012 marks the 100th anniversary of Kim Il-Sung's birth. North Korea wanted to be a strong and prosperous nation by that date, and though the military is strong, common people are hungry. The six-way diplomatic talks about North Korea's nuclear program are stalled. The North Korean people need hope for tomorrow.

God loves North Korea deeply, yet few know of his character as taught in the scriptures, his love and holiness or of Jesus' death on the cross. The church is present, but very quiet. The Lord wants to give the people hope for tomorrow and today.

Will you intercede for North Korea? Things are changing in "Chosun." Please pray through this guide to learn about the country and its people. Ask God to give you his heart for this nation. Jesus Christ is the source of hope, and he wants to offer his hope to them. We can be part of that as we pray to God for the people of North Korea. Pray with us for God's will to be done in that land for his glory and their good.

DAY 1
Roots: History of The Hermit Kingdom

From one man God made every nation of men ... God did this so that men would seek him and perhaps reach out for him and find him. Acts 17:26-27

With its 5,000 years of history, Korea is a small nation, sandwiched in between China, Japan and Russia. It was known as the "Hermit Kingdom" in the 1800s because it had little to do with most other countries. In 1866, Robert Thomas tried to take the gospel into Korea, but was martyred near Pyongyang. In 1884 the first Protestant missionaries were allowed to enter. Spreading the gospel was hard at first, but by the early 1900s, Pyongyang had so many churches that it was known as the "Jerusalem of the East."

In 1910 the Japanese occupied Korea, oppressing the people and trying to make them Japanese, but Korea kept her identity. The Great Revival of Pyongyang took place in 1907; this served to strengthen the church so she could survive the Japanese occupation. Many Korean Christians endured, keeping their identity as Christians and Koreans. Liberation Day came in 1945 at the end of World War II. Russia helped the North recover; the United States and other U.N. nations helped the South. On August 15, 1948, the Republic of Korea (ROK; South Korea) was established, followed by the founding of the Democratic People's Republic of Korea (DPRK; North Korea) on September 9 of that year. God has been working in Korea during the past 125 years; he continues to work quietly in North Korea.

FOR PRAYER

- Praise God that Korea kept her identity throughout her history of being oppressed by more powerful nations in the area.

- Pray that many people in the North would learn the history of the church there and return to the God their fathers trusted in the early 1900s.

- Pray that God will continue to work in North Korea and that Pyongyang will become a missionary-sending city!

DAY 2
Martyred for Christ

Do not be surprised at the painful trial you are suffering ... But rejoice that you participate in the sufferings of Christ, so that you may be overjoyed when his glory is revealed. 1 Peter 4:12-13

In Korea, many followers of Christ have died for their faith. During the Japanese occupation, Pastor Ju Ki-Chul was martyred in prison because of his faith in Christ and refusal to bow to the Japanese emperor.

Many other Christians were martyred during that time as well. During the Korean War, communists in South Korea martyred Pastor Son Yang-Won because of his unbending faith in Christ.

Now in North Korea, followers of Christ continue to suffer. A woman in a prison camp in the early 1990s saw eight Christian prisoners die for their faith. She screamed as she looked at the bodies and wondered, "What could be more important to them than their lives? In prison, I saw many believers die. Yet they never, never denied the God who is in heaven ... What did they see, and what am I missing?" That woman later escaped to the South and gave her life to Christ as well. *Asia News* reported that in 2010, 23 house-church Christians were arrested. Three leaders were executed and the rest were sent to Yodok prison camp. Followers of Christ are still dying for their faith in the North; and the church is still growing.

FOR PRAYER

- Praise God for the many Christians remaining faithful to him and for the growing church.
- Pray for Christians to remain firm in their faith in Christ in the midst of suffering.
- Pray that every time a disciple dies for Jesus Christ, that 10 more would come to know Christ because of his death.

DAY 3
North Korea's "Religion": Juche

"It is I who made the earth and created mankind upon it. My own hands stretched out the heavens; I marshaled their starry hosts." Isaiah 45:12

Juche (pronounced "joo-chay") means "self-reliance" and is an important concept in North Korea. Beginning in the 1960s, the government said in the Juche philosophy that they were independent and not reliant

on anyone. Juche teaches that the DPRK is the center of the world and that Kim Il-Sung and his teachings are the center of the DPRK. Juche is whatever Kim Il-Sung and his son, Kim Jong-Il, have defined it to be.

Juche is taught from kindergarten to high school. In some universities, Juche comprises up to 20-30 percent of the curriculum. Every schoolroom has two portraits at the front of the room, Kim Il-Sung and Kim Jong-Il. Those two men and the Juche philosophy are honored everywhere. It is taught to everyone, and you have to believe it (or act like you believe it).

What is the religion of the DPRK? The country claims to be atheist; but many North Korea watchers say that their god is Kim Il-Sung and Kim Jong-Il. Now, since Kim Jong-Il's death in December 2011, the government is trying to make Kim Jong-Il's son Kim Jong-Un part of the "godhead." North Koreans are taught that their purpose in life is to honor and glorify the "Great Leader" (Kim Il-Sung), the "Dear Leader" (Kim Jong-Il), and now Kim Jong-Un. What does God think of this?

FOR PRAYER

- Praise God that he is sovereign over the people of North Korea, though many do not realize it right now.

- Pray that North Koreans would hear the Word of God and learn that their purpose in life is to honor and glorify the Creator God of the Bible.

- Pray that the top leaders in the North would submit their lives to the one true God.

DAY 4
Strongholds of Sin

For our struggle is not against flesh and blood, but against the rulers, against the authorities, against the powers of this dark world. Ephesians 6:12

Along the streets in North Korea are banners that propagate the ideology of the country: "Ethnic Pride," "Our Great General Lives with Us Forever," "Safe Keep Our Way of Life," "Long Live Our Great General" and "Juche Ideology." As a foreigner passes by, the expressions on peoples' faces often show suspicion and fear. On the street and in schools, paintings are seen of North Korea crushing the American enemy; and in every office, schoolroom and public building pictures of the "Great Leader" and "Dear Leader" (Kim Il-Sung and Kim Jong-Il) appear.

These attributes of North Korea show seven of the country's spiritual strongholds: the spirit of pride, idolatry, fear and intimidation, unforgiveness, division, humanism and self-reliance. The Juche ideology states that man is the master of everything and decides his own destiny. According to Juche, North Korea stands alone (Kim Jong-Il, 1982).

However, we must look at things from God's perspective. Ephesians 6 teaches us that the real battle is spiritual. We need to pray against the evil powers in that land.

FOR PRAYER

- Praise God that he is stronger than all the spiritual strongholds in North Korea.

- Pray that the Holy Spirit will counteract the evil forces in North Korea and work through Christians who find their way across the borders.

- Pray that workers going into North Korea will show humility, love, trust, forgiveness, unity, faith in Christ and dependence upon God, and so break down the spiritual strongholds there.

DAY 5
Sick and Hungry

Bless the LORD, O my soul, and forget not all his benefits—who forgives all your sins and who heals all your diseases. Psalm 103:2-3

North Korea provides free medical treatment through its national medical service. However, the people (who call themselves the Chosun) there suffer from many significant illnesses. Since the 1990s, measles, typhus, typhoid, scarlet fever, malaria and tuberculosis have been prevalent due to poor sanitation and the weak healthcare system.

One frequent cause of disease is malnutrition. Recent information about the health of North Koreans is scarce, but many reports have documented not only substandard levels of nutrition, but also "food insecurity." An assessment by the World Food Programme (2008) stated, "Close to three quarters of respondents had reduced their food intake, over half were reportedly eating only two meals per day (down from three) and dietary diversity was extremely poor among two thirds of the surveyed population. Most North Koreans sustain themselves by consuming only maize, vegetables and wild foods—a diet lacking protein, fats and micronutrients. Food is scarcest during the 'lean season,' the five-month period prior to the autumn rice and maize harvests when stocks of the previous crops rapidly run dry."

FOR PRAYER

- Pray that God would heal their diseases (James 5:16). No matter how much knowledge, medical skills and money we have, we cannot solve the problems without God's help.

- Pray that more people would be aware of the North's health conditions. Pray for aid and skilled health professionals to reach the people, as well as solutions for the famine.

- Pray for the spiritual health of the people, that the message of the gospel can be communicated to them so they can realize new life through Christ.

DAY 6
Give Us This Day Our Daily Food

"Give us today our daily bread." Matthew 6:11

The food needs in North Korea are severe. In 2011, one-third of the children were malnourished and stunted. Five million of the 24 million people suffered from malnutrition. Most North Koreans live on 200 calories a day. At least 1,500 calories a day are needed; many people in developed countries live on twice that amount. Food conditions are at their worst since the late 1990s. Even the military and people in Pyongyang do not have enough food; these two groups are usually favored. Actually, most people eat corn because rice is not available. In times of crisis, some even eat grass from the fields.

One Christian group, Christian Friends of Korea, which works with tuberculosis (TB) patients in the North, brings greenhouse kits into the country and sets them up to help grow food for the TB patients. The late DPRK leader Kim Jong-Il wanted more fertilizer produced to help increase food production in the land.

FOR PRAYER

- Praise God for the many groups, including China and Christian businesses, which provide food for this country.

- Pray that North Korea will use its arable land wisely so as to produce food for all its citizens.

- Pray that the Lord would provide food for their bodies and food for their souls.

Many years ago, one woman who came out of the North said, "Today there are many hungry, dying people in North Korea who need not only food for their bodies, but also the Bread of Life, Jesus Christ." Let us pray for food for their bodies and for their souls.

DAY 7
A Troubled Economy

"Give me only my daily bread. Otherwise, I may have too much and … say, 'Who is the LORD?' Or I may become poor and steal, and so dishonor the name of my God." Proverbs 30:8b-9

The government said that its goal is to make Chosun (Korea) a "strong and prosperous nation" by April 15, 2012, the 100th anniversary of the birth of Kim Il-Sung, the first leader of the country. China helps the North very much. They have invested heavily into the Rajin/Sonbong area, which the DPRK has designated as a Special Economic Zone (SEZ). Eighty percent of the North's trade has been with China. North Korea wants a stronger economy; but it also wants to retain strong central political control. The Kaesong Industrial Complex near the demilitarized zone (DMZ) connects medium-sized South Korean businesses with North Korean workers. It began in 2004 and had more than 46,000 employees as of 2011. This has helped the North's economy.

The government controls the economy; it decided that military is most important, so the economy serves the military. Some estimate that about 25 percent of the DPRK gross national product goes to the military.

North Korea needs aid from other countries. However, the issue of a nuclear weapons program leaves many nations unwilling to help.

FOR PRAYER

- Praise God for the help that China and the Kaesong Industrial Complex give to North Korea's economy.

- Pray that North Korea would open up to more economic development from other countries and treat those businesses with integrity.

- Pray that the people of North Korea may be able to work and earn enough to eat and live.

DAY 8
Kim Jong-Un, the "Supreme Leader"

If a king judges the poor with fairness, his throne will always be secure.
Proverbs 29:14

On December 17, 2011, Kim Jong-Il died. His youngest son, Kim Jong-Un, was soon installed as the new leader by the party and army generals. Many years ago Kim Il-Sung picked and groomed his son Kim Jong-Il to be his successor. In September 2010, Kim Jong-Il chose Kim Jong-Un, born on January 8, 1983, to follow him. In 2010, Kim Jong-Un was promoted to the rank of four-star general and appointed vice-chairman of the Central Military Commission of the Workers Party. This is the first time that father-to-son power transfer has occurred twice in a row in a communist state.

"He thinks like his grandfather and looks like his father." This has been taught to nursery school children in the DPRK. The government wants people to give the devotion they give the first two leaders to this young man, too. Some sources say that he studied at the International School of Bern in Switzerland, an English-language school, and was an eager English learner. Sources also say that he has a strong drive to win.

A man in his late twenties is very young to rule a nation. Many North Korea watchers believe that Kim Jong-Il's brother-in-law, Jang Song-Taek, 53, and his wife Kim Kyoung-Hui, sister of Kim Jong-Il, will also play an important role in leading of the nation. They have experience—Kim Jong-Un has the name.

FOR PRAYER

- Praise God for the exposure that Kim Jong-Un has had to outside values and concepts, including freedom, fairness and morals.

- Pray that the new leader of North Korea would be the kind of leader God wants him to be.

- Pray for the salvation of Kim Jong-Un, Chang Song-Taek, Kim Kyong-Hui and other key leaders in North Korea.

DAY 9
Room for Growth

"See, I am doing a new thing! Now it springs up." Isaiah 43:19

New developments are taking place in North Korea as China paves the road into the Northeast Free Economic Zone of Rason (Rajin  and Sonbong). China has agreed to physically pave the road in exchange for the use of Rajin's port. The groundbreaking ceremony for the new road took place in June 2011. This paved mountain road into Rason will open up tremendous economic exchange and business opportunities between the two countries. North Korea, in exchange, is encouraging Chinese tourists to visit North Korea. In the summer of 2011, Chinese tourists traveled the road into Rason using their own personal vehicles for the first time. Relations between China and North Korea are strengthening.

Reasons for this close relationship with China include not only the countries' close geographic proximity, but also their common communist ideology and East Asian culture. China's investments in North Korea could allow the country to develop at a faster pace economically.

God is doing something new in North Korea. Let us pray that he continues to work, using a variety of means, including other East Asian countries.

FOR PRAYER

- Pray that China's investment in North Korea will lead to its opening. Just as China has opened to the world, pray that North Korea will open its doors.

- Pray that the economic development of North Korea will also bring new opportunities for Christian businessmen and professionals to enter and work inside North Korea.

- Pray for new, progressive policies to remove barriers for the expansion of the gospel.

DAY 10
Restless Hearts

Find rest, O my soul, in God alone; my hope comes from him. He alone is my rock and my salvation. Psalm 62:5-6a

Most people in North Korea are hungry for physical food. They also have spiritual needs; their need for God and meaning in life is even more important.

North Korea is officially a communist, atheist nation. Yet the people still need some power beyond themselves that gives them hope. God made human beings with a God-shaped vacuum. "Our hearts are restless until they find their rest in You (God)," said Augustine. It seems that the North Korean government is trying

to fill that vacuum with Kim Il-Sung and Kim Jong-Il. One Korean from the North said, "The North Korean government has established policies to instill in the North Korean psyche the idea that the Great Leader (Kim Il-Sung) is absolute and divine. In a multitude of ways, these policies are implemented thoroughly, uniformly and absolutely." The government teaches the people that the Great Leader provides all their needs. The system tries to fill their spiritual needs with humans; but God knows that these needs can be filled by himself alone. The Bible says, "They ... worshiped and served created things rather than the Creator" (Romans 1:25). Let us pray that their hearts will be restless and that they will seek until they find the God of the Bible.

FOR PRAYER

- Praise God for the God-consciousness that he has placed within the hearts of the North Korean people.

- Pray that the people would sense a need for God and continue to seek him until they find him.

- Pray that people would sense that human leaders are inadequate substitutes for the God they need.

DAY 11
Dwelling Among the People

The Word became flesh and made his dwelling among us. We have seen his glory, the glory of the One and Only, who came from the Father, full of grace and truth. John 1:14

As General Director of China Inland Mission for 35 years, D.E. Hoste was an example of a godly servant—prayerful, humble and self-effacing.

A classic photo shows him dressed as a typical Chinese peasant and enjoying a simple Chinese meal with a local person in the street. He set as his life goal "to live to be forgotten in order that Christ will be remembered." Many people did forget his name, but they were greatly challenged by his humble life and example, which pointed them to Christ.

The word "dwelling" in John 1 comes from the same root word as "sanctuary," "tabernacle" and "tent" in the Old Testament. "Dwelling" refers to God's presence with his people and speaks of his accessibility. "Sanctuary," or "tabernacle," emphasizes the character of the place where God's holiness and glory were proclaimed. The "tent" emphasizes God's identification with his people who were living in tents. All these intentions were fulfilled by our Lord Jesus Christ.

In bringing the gospel to the unreached peoples, we need to follow the Lord's example of incarnational ministry. This is especially true when serving in North Korea where our lives speak louder than our words and actions.

FOR PRAYER

- Praise God that a small number of workers are now residing or traveling regularly inside North Korea.

- Pray for these workers to follow the Lord's example and exercise an incarnational ministry among the North Korean people and officials.

- Pray that the seeds of the gospel will be sown and grow in the hearts of North Korean guides, officials, patients, professionals and students.

DAY 12
Train Up a Child

But Jesus called the children to him and said, "Let the little children come to me, and do not hinder them, for the kingdom of God belongs to such as these." Luke 18:16

From nursery school, children in North Korea are taught that Kim Il-Sung and Kim Jong-Il provide all their needs. Portraits of the "Great Leader" and the "Dear Leader" are at the front of every classroom. One man said that he felt as if the two leaders were watching how he studied. The schools also have a special room with the portraits. Each week a selected student takes care of that room, wearing special slippers and using a special cloth to dust the portraits regularly. Children learn the history of the two leaders' childhoods and famous places they visited.

Arithmetic word problems have to do with war, particularly the Korean War: "During the Korean War, 564 Chinese fighters and 45 Russian fighters joined ... 789 fighters from the [DPRK] to repel the invasions of the [soldiers] of South Korea. How many fighters are there in all?" What do you think little boys think about in light of that?

God teaches in the Bible that parents should teach their children about God and his law starting at a young age. People remember as adults what they were taught as children. Let us pray for the children of North Korea and their hearts and minds.

FOR PRAYER

- Praise God that he loves the children of North Korea.
- Pray that God would protect their minds so they can rightfully evaluate the values they are taught.
- Pray that at home parents would teach their children values of truth, honesty and curiosity.

DAY 13
Church in Hiding

"And on this rock I will build my church, and the gates of Hades will not overcome it." Matthew 16:18

We do not hear much about the church of Jesus Christ in the North. The government leaders do not want people to know much about the church, but she is alive. The DPRK government claims that there is religious freedom. Two Protestant churches controlled by the government exist in the capital, and they may have some genuine believers. However, most true disciples belong to quiet house churches throughout the land.

Some "church services" in the North consist of two believers quietly meeting in one of their homes, sharing scripture they have memorized, discussing it and praying together. Pray that these churches will grow in faith and in living out the faith.

One source said many people have become followers of the Lord Jesus in the last few years. One dear lady even sent out a written testimony of her transformed allegiance.

Another source also claimed that mp3 players with soul-nourishing scriptures are getting into the country. Pray for the gospel to continue to enter the country and people's hearts; and pray for the church to grow in depth, quality, influence and number. When the North opens up, we will be amazed and humbled at the depth of the faith we see in North Korean disciples.

FOR PRAYER

- Praise God that the church of Jesus Christ is growing in the North, despite opposition to it.

- Pray that the believers can encourage each other in the quiet house churches throughout the land.

- Pray that the Word of God will continue to get into the land and into people's hands, building up the church and drawing seekers to the Lord Jesus.

DAY 14
Suffering for the Gospel

In fact, everyone who wants to live a godly life in Christ Jesus will be persecuted. 2 Timothy 3:12

The church in North Korea is growing and also suffering. Many years ago, elementary school teachers said to their students, "Tell us if your parents have a black book at home that they often read in private." The children who reported their parents never saw them again.

The government also does not want people to learn of Christians suffering for their faith; if they learned of that, they would wonder why they persevere.

The Christians in North Korea know they have to suffer for the Lord. Some composed a confession of faith entitled, "A Code of Conduct for the Warriors of Christ:"

1) A person who believes in Jesus will incur the contempt of others.

2) People who believe in Jesus will experience suffering.

3) Before you learn how to receive compliments, learn how to take insults!

4) The people who believe in our Jesus wipe away the tears of the people who don't know him as well as the tears of one another. We must become comforters to all who experience suffering.

5) Love fosters love in others. We must love others with the love of Jesus; then they will become followers of Jesus.

6) Before anything else, we must live according to the Bible as our measuring stick.

FOR PRAYER

- Praise God that the church is growing as people see how she handles suffering.

- Pray that believers will stand firm in their faith in Christ, whatever treatment they receive.

- Pray that the church in the North will grow because she is suffering for the Lord Jesus.

DAY 15
The "Great Leader," Kim Il-Sung

Therefore God … gave him the name that is above every name, that… every tongue confess that Jesus Christ is Lord, to the glory of God the Father. Philippians 2:9-11

Kim Il-Sung was regarded as the "Great Leader." The government teaches that, "the Great Leader's spirit is always with us, and he demands our respect at all times because he has done so much for the country."

Kim Il-Sung was born on April 15, 1912, making April 15, 2012 the hundredth anniversary of his birth. April 15 is the biggest holiday in the DPRK. The government wants 2012 to be the biggest celebration of all, and for the DPRK to become a "strong and prosperous nation" by then to honor its Great Leader.

Ironically, Kim Il-Sung comes from a Christian background. His grandfather was a minister, his father an elder and his mother a deaconess. Kim himself was a church organist at one time.

Kim Il-Sung did lead his nation out of poverty after World War II. He taught everyone that the DPRK relied on itself and himself. Now he is honored by all. He chose his son Kim Jong-Il to succeed him. When Kim Il-Sung died in 1994, most citizens thought that god had died. The son, Kim Jong-Il, linked himself solidly with his father so as to receive similar honor. Kim Il-Sung is now honored as the Eternal President.

FOR PRAYER

- Praise God that Jesus Christ's name is above every name.
- Pray that many in North Korea will have doubts about giving honor to one who is no longer alive.
- Pray that North Koreans will honor the Creator God more than they honor any human being.

DAY 16
The "Dear Leader," Kim Jong-Il

They replied, "If today you will be a servant to these people and serve them and give them a favorable answer, they will always be your servants." 1 Kings 12:7

Kim Jong-Il, referred to as the "Dear Leader," ruled the country from 1994 to 2011. He passed away suddenly on December 17, 2011 at the age of 69. Kim Il-Sung, his father, chose Kim Jong-Il in the 1970s to be his successor. He emphasized "military first." He wanted the military to be loyal to him. After Kim Il-Sung died in 1994, the economy declined in the North. Famines hit in the late 1990s, and many people starved from malnutrition. The food situation has recently become very dire again.

Around August 2008, Kim Jong-Il suffered a stroke. In 2010, Kim Jong-Il announced that his youngest son, Kim Jong-Un, would be his successor. Since December 2011, Kim Jong-Un has been recognized as the leader of the nation. Many believe that he will observe a three-year period of mourning for his father, as Kim Jong-Il did for his father. Many observers think things will be quiet with no major changes during this time.

Recently the public has had more access to news from the outside. CDs, radios and VCRs are seeping across the Chinese border more and more. If the people inside have news of the outside, it will be harder for Kim Jong-Un and the government to exercise complete control. May a wise leader rule this nation!

FOR PRAYER

- Praise God that he is sovereign over all nations and leaders in this world.
- Pray that there will be a smooth transfer of leadership in North Korea after Kim Jong-Il's death.
- Pray for change after his death, change for the good of his people.

DAY 17
More Than Business

Where there are no oxen, the manger is empty, but from the strength of an ox comes an abundant harvest. Proverbs 14:4

Besides Pyongyang, three special economic zones (SEZs) allow foreign companies to operate: Rajin-Sonbong (Rason), in the far northeast corner, just 50 kilometers from China; an area near Sinuiju, a large city on the southwestern border with China (three-fourths of all trade between those two countries passes here); and Kaesong, on the border between North and South Korea.

The North Korean government wants to develop these economic zones. However, this does not mean they cooperate in allowing them to operate efficiently. To control the influence of the SEZs, the government carefully manages access by both citizens and foreigners. They hope that small areas of controlled capitalism will generate significant amounts of income.

Rason's main advantage is its link to the sea which helps save substantial transportation costs. Kaesong is viable because the South Korean government supports it. Sinuiju is mostly about low labor costs for Chinese companies.

Overall, these SEZs are good for the DPRK. People can earn a living and also learn of the outside world.

FOR PRAYER

- Praise God for these special economic zones where international businessmen can enter North Korea.

- Pray that Christians will take advantage of these opportunities and make up a large percentage of the business people living and working inside the DPRK.

- Pray that Christian international businessmen can model hard, honest work ethics and also be light and salt for the Lord Jesus.

DAY 18
Teachers, Role Models

The LORD gives wisdom, and from his mouth come knowledge and understanding. Proverbs 2:6

Approximately 10-15 percent of North Korean high school students go to college where they study for four to six years. Many study science and mathematics, but much time is also spent on political studies, social education and "voluntary labor."

Like many Asian countries, education is highly valued and teachers are greatly respected. College students are usually very thankful for their education and want to study well in order to be able to contribute to the development of the country.

FOR PRAYER

- Pray for students in universities throughout the DPRK to think about the education they receive and grow to be those who can truly contribute to the welfare of their country.

- Pray for foreign teachers already working in the DPRK to be given much wisdom, to be excellent professionals in their work and to be granted favor in the eyes of the authorities.

- Pray for more foreigners to be willing to work in the area of education for the benefit of the North Korean people.

In recent years, the main foreign language taught changed from Russian to English, so there has been a greater demand for foreign teachers, both to teach English and to train local teachers. They also seem more open to outside expertise in areas such as computing, agriculture and even management and finance. Many opportunities are open for well-qualified foreigners to provide short-term teacher training, seminars or longer term teaching at some universities.

DAY 19
Practical Need, Spiritual Impact

"The King will reply, 'I tell you the truth, whatever you did for one of the least of these brothers of mine, you did for me.'" Matthew 25:40

NGO (non-governmental organization) work is primarily related to food, education and health. Just as Jesus cared for people's physical

needs, NGO workers are also touching people's lives.

NGOs are not only providing supplies, but also establishing relationships with local residents as they visit villages and supply food or medicine to hospitals and childcare centers. Through all this, God's love can also enter these villages. Local residents know that the rice and medicine from many of these NGOs are not from their leader. Many express thanks to the NGO workers.

"We pray on behalf of those who cannot pray. We praise on behalf of those who cannot praise. We feel that God is working in the land; and that it will not be long until the glory of God shines upon that place. As we enter the land and serve them as worshipers with God's love, the people are beginning to be changed. They begin to think, to feel and to perceive that there are some discrepancies from what they have learned and known before." (from and NGO worker)

FOR PRAYER

- Pray that Christian NGO workers in North Korea will do their work "as unto the Lord" despite many practical challenges.

- Pray that Christian NGO workers will show God's love in practical ways and that God will change people's lives.

- Pray that Christian NGO workers will contribute to God's kingdom in North Korea through their supplies, service and prayers.

DAY 20
An Open Door

"I know your deeds. See, I have placed before you an open door that no one can shut." Revelation 3:8

Sarah was trained as an English teacher and felt a strong burden to use her profession for God. She discovered a need for English teachers in North Korea and was drawn to it. She found an agency that places professionals there. She went and studied the Korean language for two years, taught for two years in another country, upgraded her qualifications and now is teaching in North Korea.

She enjoys working with these students who are eager to learn. One student wrote, "I see Sarah as my model." Sarah felt fulfilled as a teacher and was glad to help these students who would one day become leaders in the DPRK.

God has opened the door for us to use our professional skills to serve him. Like other creative-access nations, the DPRK restricts the entry of Christian missionaries. It does welcome, though, Christian professionals who are willing to use their skills to help North Korea develop.

These professionals need a visa to legally enter. They need academic qualifications, marketable skills and work experience. They need training to be effective cross-cultural workers. They witness by being people of integrity, doing a professional job well and sharing the news of Christ with sensitivity. Professional service in the spirit of Christ is a great way to contextualize the gospel in both word and deed.

FOR PRAYER

- Praise God for many open doors for Christian professionals to use their skills to bless North Korea. Pray that these doors will continue to open.

- Pray that many Christian professionals will be willing to walk through these doors.

- Pray for Christian professionals in North Korea who are always being watched and are isolated from much spiritual fellowship and the outside world, as well as facing constant spiritual warfare.

DAY 21
Poised for Impact

For we are to God the aroma of Christ among those who are being saved and those who are perishing. 2 Corinthians 2:15

Many Chinese in northeast China are Korean-Chinese, that is, ethnically Korean and politically citizens of China. These people know both Korean and Chinese languages. "Chosun-jok" is the Korean word for these people; Chosun is an old name for Korea and what North Korea calls itself. The Chosun-jok have access to North Korea. They can go in and out easily for business or tourist reasons. The Korean they speak is very similar to the Korean spoken inside. (North Korean language and South Korean language are different; language reflects culture, and the cultures in the North and South have become very different in the last 60 years.) The Chosun-jok also live in a communist country; hence, they understand North Korea better than people from capitalist nations (including South Korea) do.

Some of the Korean-Chinese people use escaping North Koreans for selfish purposes, such as laborers or as wives for Chinese men who cannot find wives. Some of the Korean-Chinese, however, are Christians and care deeply for the spiritual welfare of North Koreans. Some of these Chinese citizens can go in to the DPRK for business purposes. They can be salt and light for the Lord Jesus. Salt and light are quiet but have a deep impact. Pray that the aroma of Christ will go forth from Korean-Chinese Christians.

FOR PRAYER

- Praise God for the Korean-Chinese disciples in northeast China.

- Pray that Korean-Chinese believers will model Christian principles in their businesses.

- Pray that many Korean-Chinese Christians will be mobilized and equipped to go into North Korea on business and be salt and light for Jesus.

DAY 22
The Story of a "Zainichi"

"In your hearts set apart Christ as Lord. Always be prepared to give an answer to everyone who asks you to give the reason for the hope that you have." 1 Peter 3:15

Although living in Japan, Sung attended a pro-North Korea school when he was young. He is part of a large number of "Zainichi," a term referring to ethnic Koreans who live in Japan. Some identify with North Korea. Perhaps more than 900,000 Zainichi live in Japan.

Sung attended the North Korean-run Chosun School, where all teaching is done in Korean and pro-North Korea ideology is a large part of the curriculum. He also had the opportunity to go to the pro-North Chosun University. However, he wanted to study medicine, a subject that university did not offer and ended up attending elsewhere. Sung eventually changed his citizenship from North to South Korea.

FOR PRAYER

- Praise God that the Zainichi Koreans in Japan have religious freedom; pray that many more of them will hear the gospel and trust and follow Jesus Christ.

- Pray that Christians reaching out to North Koreans will respect them as people.

- Pray that some of these Koreans in Japan may catch a vision for the spiritual needs of people in North Korea.

During college, Sung met a Korean Christian who invited him to church. Sung had never known about church before, but he enjoyed the fellowship and was moved by the sermon. Later, he began studying the Bible and was baptized. He's now attending seminary. Although he had some connections with North Korea, Sung does not have a special burden for the Zainichi or North Koreans. Instead, he wants to be a witness "to all people."

DAY 23
North Korea's "Big Brother"

"Away with the noise of your songs! I will not listen to the music of your harps. But let justice roll on like a river, righteousness like a never-failing stream!" Amos 5:23-24

C hina is one ally, "big brother" and friend that the DPRK still has. They are linked politically and economically. Before the Korean War, when the communists in China were fighting in China's civil war, North Korean communist soldiers provided great help. In turn, during the Korean War,  China greatly helped North Korea. In March 2010, the DPRK agreed to let China use the port of Rajin, on its northeast border, for 10 years. China agreed to pour millions of dollars of investment into the area. It is mutually beneficial, since China now has use of a northeast port on the Sea of Japan.

The DPRK government has been looking closely at how China has developed its market. China gradually shed state control of the economy to become one of the world's biggest economies; North Korea has kept its rigid system. It seems like the North wants the benefits that China has but is not willing to pay the price.

China has continued to help North Korea. One reason could be that the DPRK is a comfortable buffer zone of communism (that China has much influence over) between China and South Korea, as well as U.S. forces in South Korea and Japan.

FOR PRAYER

- Praise God that China is helping North Korea, providing food and trading with them.

- Pray that the DPRK and China will relate in mature, mutually respectful ways.

- Pray that China, who has an economic relationship with many nations in the world, will help the DPRK also relate economically with many of those nations.

DAY 24
Same, But Different

He has showed you, O man, what is good. And what does the Lord require of you? To act justly and to love mercy and to walk humbly with your God. Micah 6:8

The relationship between North Korea and South Korea is very important and also very sensitive. A united Korea was divided between 1945 and 1950. Both nations want reunification on their own terms. For 10 years, two South Korean presidents followed the "Sunshine Policy" and gave much aid to the North. In 2008, a new president was installed in South Korea, leading to changes in the South's North Korean policies. This led to a worsening of relations between the two nations. In 2010 the North and South clashed in

two incidents, with the sinking of a South Korean military ship (possibly caused by a DPRK torpedo); and fire being exchanged near an island west of the demilitarized zone (DMZ) in which some people were killed. Both nations are important and could help each other. For example, middle-size businesses from the South have built factories in Kaesong, North Korea near the DMZ; the South provides capital and the North provides labor.

The two nations have one history but are now divided, with two different cultures. Values, government, economy, religion and even language, to some degree, are different. These differences present challenges for believers as they seek the Lord for his desires and outcomes.

FOR PRAYER

- Praise God for the Kaesong Industrial Complex and other ways these two nations are cooperating.
- Pray that the church of Christ in the South will show the love of Christ to each other and to people from the North.
- Pray for believers as they seek God's will for the Korean peninsula.

DAY 25
North Korea on the Global Stage

Righteousness exalts a nation, but sin is a disgrace to any people. Proverbs 14:34

North Korea claims to be self-reliant and self-sufficient. In actuality, it, like every nation, needs other nations. It has a good relationship with other communist countries, especially China. And for the most part, it has good relationships with formerly communist nations. It has diplomatic relationships with 160 nations, including Australia, Singapore, the Philippines, the Netherlands, the United Kingdom, Germany and Canada. Twenty nations have consulates in the DPRK.

The DPRK wants help and investment in many areas, including business, health care and education. In 2011, the European Union offered 10 million pounds worth of food aid to the DPRK, with the condition that it be monitored so that it reaches needy people. Many NGO groups work quietly inside.

It takes a long time to gain trust in the North. When visitors first enter the country, at least two guides accompany them wherever they go. By going in many times over two or three years through business or education and applying for residence permits, they gain more trust from the government and are granted more freedom; they can eventually function without the guides. The North Korean government needs wisdom in relating to international leaders.

FOR PRAYER

- Praise God that so many nations have diplomatic relations with the DPRK.

- Pray for Christians from the nations listed above to go and serve the country in various ways and be light and salt for the Lord Jesus.

- Pray that the leaders of the DPRK will be wise in relating with international leaders and do so in healthy and honest ways.

DAY 26
Wanted: Christian Professionals

"The harvest is plentiful but the workers are few. Ask the Lord of the harvest, therefore, to send out workers into his harvest field."
Matthew 9:37-38

North Korea is looking for professional expertise. These opportunities are open to Christians. What kind of workers would thrive? They need to be solid disciples, pioneers who live lives of integrity. They need to be well-qualified in their field. They need to persevere in language learning and in working in a country that has very different values than most other countries. They need to be people who want to live incarnationally, learning much about the culture and values of the land and seeking to be light and salt for the Light of the world. They need to accept very basic living conditions. They have to be in excellent health.

People who intend to work in North Korea will face many difficulties. They will need much patience during the waiting times. They will need to endure times of isolation. They will need to be willing to take family into these circumstances and also endure some times of separation from family. They will have to endure times of being watched by the government. They will need to be people of prayer who can engage in spiritual warfare, depending on the Lord. They will need to be ready to suffer. They will also feel immense joy at helping a country professionally and spiritually that needs the gospel.

FOR PRAYER

- Praise God that some Christian professionals are working in North Korea.

- Pray that the Lord would call many more Christian professionals to be equipped and sent to North Korea.

- Pray that they would endure and be effective in doing the work that the Lord wants them to do there.

DAY 27
Escape to the South

"Love your neighbor as yourself. I am the LORD." Leviticus 19:18b

Many people from the North are escaping. If they go to China, they are considered "illegal" and China usually sends them back. Most would like to go to South Korea. More than 23,000 people have arrived in the South since 1953, with about 22,000 of them arriving since 2000. These people are referred to as *"talbukja"* (pronounced tahl-boog-jah), people who have escaped the north and are accepted by the South Korea government.

Though the North and South share a 5,000-year history and the same basic language, many things are very different. The *talbukja* in the South are most aware of this. One government is communist; one is democratic. One economy is controlled by the state; one is capitalist. One nation is focused on the leaders; the other is increasingly individualistic. Even the languages have become different. The South uses quite a bit of English or combinations of Korean and English. Language in the North reflects its communist influence and social structure. Religion is very different; the DPRK is officially atheistic, and the South has religious freedom with many Buddhists and Christians. Even the food is different in the South. All these factors make it hard for *talbukja* to adjust to life in the South.

FOR PRAYER

- Praise God that many *talbukja* are coming to South Korea where they can freely hear the gospel.

- Pray that *talbukja* will be able to adjust to the new culture in the South and that many South Koreans will kindly and respectfully help them adjust.

- Pray that South Korean Christians will show the love of Christ to the *talbukja* in practical ways.

DAY 28
Adjusting to Life in South Korea

Let no debt remain outstanding, except the continuing debt to love one another, for he who loves his fellowman has fulfilled the law.
Romans 13:8

More than 23,000 people from North Korea have come to South Korea, but they find it hard to fit in. The South Korean government is trying to help these new citizens in many ways; it realizes that helping them will help with reunification in the future.

Many years ago, the South Korean government set up Hanawon, a resettlement center for people from the North. At Hanawon, the newcomers learn about personal finance, health and language differences in the South, the social and political culture of the South and practical

things such as computers and ATM machines. After they leave Hanawon, they receive some money for basic housing. The government is helping with counseling centers to help them handle their unique stresses. Some of these counselors are from North Korea as well. The South Korean government increasingly recognizes the role that those from the North have in helping others who come. In 2011, a man from the North was selected by the government to teach South Koreans about reunification and help prepare them for its coming. He said that people from the North understand the North and can best teach South Koreans about the North. Praise God that the South Korean government is actively involved in helping.

FOR PRAYER

- Praise the Lord that the South Korean government is helping people from the North adjust.

- Pray that the South Korean government will help wisely and respect those from the North as precious citizens.

- Pray that other South Koreans will respect the newcomers and help them in practical ways, such as finding jobs and job training.

DAY 29
Ministry to Talbukja

To the Jews I became like a Jew, to win the Jews ... I have become all things to all men so that by all possible means I might save some.
1 Corinthians 9:20, 22

Although some South Koreans do not help those from the North (called *talbukja*, see Day 27) to adjust, many others do. Some churches and Christian groups are reaching out to these new citizens. Some *talbukja* churches led by *talbukja* pastors have formed. Some who come are meeting Jesus Christ, attending seminary and ministering to others like them.

One group started "Yeomyeong (Day of New Dawning) School" in Seoul in 2004. Several churches support it. It helps young people from the North finish high school-level studies so they can enter college. It also provides a Christian, warm, friendly and fun atmosphere. If needed, the school helps the young person finish middle school level studies first. In 2010 the school was recognized by the government as an alternative high school for *talbukja* students. In 2011, the school had 70-75 students enrolled. The students often go on field trips to see more of the nation and famous sites in the South. Praise God for this and similar schools, and pray that he will help them persevere in this important ministry.

FOR PRAYER

- Praise the Lord for the many South Korean Christian groups reaching out to *talbukja*.

- Pray that more South Korean Christians would lovingly reach out and help these people.

- Pray that South Koreans ministering to *talbukja* would remember that they come from a different cultural background.

DAY 30
Food for Their Souls: The Bible

"As the rain and the snow come down from heaven, and do not return to it without watering the earth … so is my word that goes out from my mouth." Isaiah 55:10-11

A woman who spent six years in a labor camp wrote: "It is nice to send rice to North Korea … yet today there are many hungry, dying people in North Korea who need not only food for their bodies, but also the Bread of Life, Jesus Christ".

The Bible is available only at the four registered churches in the DPRK, so distributing God's Word is a challenge. There are other creative ways to deliver the gospel message. A few people have hidden a radio in their homes—that is not tuned to the state channel—and heard Christian radio and Bible readings from the outside. Many believers hand copied what they have heard from the radio and made up their own Bible. One Christian in South Korea wanted to share the Christmas story with some North Koreans who had gotten out. She realized that she could not start at Matthew; she had to start at Genesis. Most North Koreans have no idea of the content of the Bible. Hence, using the chronological Bible storytelling approach would work well, explaining God, creation and how he has worked in history up to Jesus.

With the Bibles in their hands, believers will know Almighty God and his will for all people, including North Koreans.

FOR PRAYER

- Praise God that Christians inside North Korea have access to the Word of God.
- Pray that the Bible will enter the North—through print, audio, radio or whatever means.
- Pray that as the Bible is read, that the Word would bring conviction and repentance.

DAY 31
Prayer: The Key to Revival

"If my people … will humble themselves and pray and seek my face and turn from their wicked ways, then will I hear from heaven and will forgive their sin and will heal their land." 2 Chronicles 7:14

The revival in Korea in 1907 was characterized by confession of sins among missionaries, which spread to the local Christians. Also, people realized anew the power of prevailing prayer. People everywhere were deeply convicted of sin. This was followed by confession, restitution and audible prayer en masse—a new way of praying, which has since become common among Korean Christians.

Just as Pentecost in Acts 2 was preceded by a prayer movement, revival in North Korea will be keyed by a prayer movement of Christians from around the world. God is looking for informed intercessors that unite in persevering prayer for the nation and the people in North Korea. Many prayer groups for North Korea have been established in many churches, cities and countries.

This is a critical time for North Korea as it prepares for new leadership and yet faces deepening humanitarian, social, economic and spiritual needs. Let us pray together for God's healing upon this nation, and for North Korea to rise up to be a blessing to the nations.

FOR PRAYER

- Praise God for an emerging worldwide prayer movement for North Korea through the publication of prayer resources and formation of prayer groups and prayer networks.

- Pray that many more Christians will use the prayer resources available to help them become effective intercessors for North Korea.

- Pray that we will see a breakthrough in the spiritual strongholds that bind this nation and the hearts of the people, and a turning to the living God.

NEXT STEPS

If God is leading you to involvement with his purposes in North Korea, consider the following options:

1) Pray - Use this booklet and other materials to intercede for North Korea on a regular basis. Write *northkoreanews@omfmail.com* and ask for the bi-monthly prayer bulletin which provides fresh news and daily prayer points. Form or join a small group to pray for North Korea each month. Download a map of the Korean peninsula and put it near your desk or prayer corner as a reminder to pray.

2) Go - Visit northeast Asia and see the land of North Korea on a Serve Asia trip. As noted in this prayer guide, there are ways to go and serve in North Korea as highly qualified professionals. Consider using your professional skills to serve in North Korea. Contact us to learn more.

3) Welcome - Reach out to Koreans in your neighborhood. There are many Korean restaurants and churches in which you could build relationships.

4) Mobilize - Order one of these booklets for a friend or your church. Start a prayer group for North Korea. Be an advocate for God's work.

5) Learn - Explore news sites and books related to North Korea. Two good ones are *Nothing to Envy* by Barbara Demick and *Great Leader, Dear Leader* by Bertil Linter. Watch the DVD *Crossing*, a true-to-life movie about North Korea and a young family there.

6) Send - Partner with organizations or Christians working in North Korea through the sharing of your time, money and other resources.

For more information on how you can be involved, go to www.omf.org.

*Source list available upon request.

TIMELINE

1866 Robert Thomas, first missionary to Korea, is killed.

1884 Protestant missionaries allowed to enter Korea.

1907 Revival in Pyongyang.

1910 Korea comes under Japanese rule.

1945 After World War II, Japanese occupation of Korea ends with Soviet troops occupying the North, and U.S. troops the South.

1946 North Korea's Communist Party inaugurated. Soviet-backed leadership installed, including Red Army-trained Kim Il-Sung.

1948 Democratic People's Republic of Korea proclaimed. Soviet troops withdraw. South declares independence.

1950 North invades.

1953 Armistice ends Korean War, which cost 2 million lives.

1991 North and South Korea join the United Nations.

1994 Death of Kim Il-Sung. Kim Jong-Il succeeds him as leader of North Korea.

1996 Severe famine follows widespread floods. As many as 1 million North Koreans die between 1996-99.

2003 Six-nation talks in Beijing on North Korea's nuclear program begin.

2006 North Korea claims to test a nuclear weapon for the first time.

2010 Sinking of South Korean warship, allegedly by the North, raises tensions on the peninsula to new heights.

Kim Jong-Il's youngest son Kim Jong-Un is appointed to senior political and military posts, fueling speculation that he is being prepared to succeed his father.

2011 Kim Jong-Il dies on December 17. Kim Jong-Un presides at the funeral, is hailed as "Great Successor" and takes over from his father as chairman of the National Defense Commission.

2012 Army pledges loyalty to Kim Jong-Un in a mass parade held to mark the 70th anniversary of Kim Jong-Il's birth.